Harvesttime

Wheat

By Inez Snyder

Welcome Books™

Children's Press®
A Division of Scholastic Inc.
New York / Toronto / London / Auckland / Sydney
Mexico City / New Delhi / Hong Kong
Danbury, Connecticut

Photo Credits: Cover © Darrell Gulin/Corbis; p. 5 © Kevin Fleming/Corbis; p. 7 © Chinch Gryniewicz/Corbis; p. 9 © FK Photo/Corbis; p. 11 © COLOR-PIC/Animals Animals/Earth Scenes; pp. 13, 15 © Richard Hamilton Smith/Corbis; p. 17 © Dave Schiefelbein/Getty Images, Inc.; p. 19 © Corbis; p. 21 © Fukuhara, Inc./Corbis

Contributing Editors: Shira Laskin and Jennifer Silate
Book Design: Erica Clendening

Library of Congress Cataloging-in-Publication Data

Snyder, Inez.
    Wheat / by Inez Snyder.
    p. cm.—(Harvesttime)
    Summary: Introduces wheat, from the time it is planted in a field until
    it is made into different foods.
    Includes bibliographical references and index.
    ISBN 0-516-27596-8 (lib. bdg.) — ISBN 0-516-25915-6 (pbk.)
    1. Wheat—Juvenile literature. 2. Wheat—Harvesting—Juvenile
    literature. [1. Wheat. 2. Harvesting.] I. Title. II. Series.

SB191.W5S714 2004
633.1′15—dc21
                                              2003010811

Contents

Wheat is planted in **fields**.

5

Wheat is green when it starts to grow.

Wheat turns a golden color when it is ready to be **harvested**.

Farmers use **machines** to harvest wheat.

11

The machines have
big **blades**.

The blades cut the wheat.

13

The machines pick up
the wheat after it is cut.

Then they put the wheat in
a big truck.

The truck takes the wheat to large bins.

The wheat is kept in the bins.

People use the **grains** from the wheat plant to make food.

19

Wheat is used to make many different foods.

New Words

blades (**blaydz**) the cutting parts of something

fields (**feeldz**) flat, open areas of land without trees or buildings

grains (**graynz**) tiny seeds of rice, corn, wheat, or other plants that are used for growing new plants or are eaten

harvested (**hahr**-vuhst-uhd) picked or gathered

machines (muh-**sheenz**) things that are made to do work or to help make other things

wheat (**hweet**) a tall grass plant that is used to make flour, pasta, and some kinds of breakfast cereal

To Find Out More

Books
Wheat
by Elaine Landau
Grolier Publishing Co., Inc.

The Wheat We Eat
by Allan Fowler
Grolier Publishing Co., Inc.

Web Site
Wheat Mania!
http://www.wheatmania.com
This Web site has a lot of information about wheat, including the history of wheat, how wheat is harvested, and what life is like on a wheat farm.

Index

About the Author

Inez Snyder has written several books to help children learn to read. She also enjoys cooking for her family.

Reading Consultants

Kris Flynn, Coordinator, Small School District Literacy, The San Diego County Office of Education

Shelly Forys, Certified Reading Recovery Specialist, W.J. Zahnow Elementary School, Waterloo, IL

Paulette Mansell, Certified Reading Recovery Specialist, and Early Literacy Consultant, TX